You Can't Make This Stuff Up

RIDICULOUSLY FUNNY STORIES BY REAL COPS

Retold by:

Mike The Cop, Elizabeth Shiftwell, and

David R. Edwards

CONTENTS

PREFACE

The stories you've all been waiting for...

By far, when cops end up in conversations with people that know they're a cop, they will inevitably be asked one of two main questions: "What's the scariest situation you've ever been in?" and "What's the funniest or craziest thing you've ever seen?"

While we would never want to, nor should we ever, minimize the very serious side to the job of law enforcement, we've found that humor is a great tool for building bridges between cops and non-cops. It is one of the simplest ways to communicate that we're really all the same at the end of the day in that we are *gasp*: *human*.

It is this concept that leads us at www.HumanizingTheBadge.com to work so hard to be an excellent representative of those who support law enforcement and those that put themselves on the line for each of us every single day without hesitation. We have written in great detail about the many serious issues facing law enforcement today, but for this brief book we decided to show the lighter side of things, which are plenteous!

We asked cops from all over to submit their stories of crazy or funny situations, dispatched runs and even weird things they've found in the pockets of people they encounter. What resulted was this book that we hope you'll read and laugh with; re-read and laugh some more; share it with a friend who will also laugh and on and on it will go.

As we prepare this book in early 2016, there is an overwhelming perception in major media that is "anti-cop." However, we don't buy into it. Beneath the layer of foam that is that hateful rhetoric and distorted perception, we know the substance is that most people are law abiding citizens who are deeply thankful for their local, regional and federal law enforcement officers doing the tough work of keeping them safe, even when they don't do it perfectly, because remember: we're human.

Ultimately, this book is for you, the perpetual and consistent supporter of those willing to risk it all. But perhaps you are on the fence about how you feel about cops and this will get you to crack a smile and maybe open up to the idea that we have more in common than you think. Maybe, just maybe, being on the same page isn't as far off as some people would have us to believe.

YOU CAN'T MAKE THIS STUFF UP

I'M WATCHING POOORRRN!

A couple weeks ago my partner and I were out "huntin'" on patrol and we entered this park that's nothing but a gathering place for sugar honey iced tea heads (aka, drug addicts). As we pulled in, we saw a truck that we recognized. The owner of the truck is well known by all of us, and we've locked him up before. He's got his head down and he's slouched forward. We figured he was shooting up or just got done and is nodding off.

I approached on the driver's side as my partner came up on the other side. As I reached the cab, I saw that this guy's got no pants on, holding his phone in one hand watching porn and going to town on himself with the other. Broad daylight! Not what I was expecting. I asked him what he's doing, and without even looking up he mumbles "watching porn". I said, "what?" I'm still surprised by what I'm seeing as he yells at me, "I'm watching pooorrrn!!" At this point he looked up and saw the word POLICE plastered on my chest. As soon as he does, he dives across the front bench of his truck onto the passenger side where my partner is standing, grabs a nice sized baggie of crack and tries to eat it. My partner grabbed his arm trying to keep him from doing so. I was trying to grab his other arm while his legs are flailing in my face. MIND YOU, HE STILL HAS NO PANTS ON! I take a kick to the chest (had my vest on, no biggie, although the fact that he was barefoot makes it a biggie). I grabbed a leg, pulled him out of the truck. He's trying to hang on, so I had to "gently assist" him to the grassy area next to where his truck was parked. As I was "guiding" him from the cab of his truck to the grass, a girthy, veiny, dildo comes shooting out of - I think you know where . . .. Just when I thought I'd seen it all . . ..

When all was said and done, there were no officers injured, the crack was recovered, and the suspect booked accordingly. And it just so happens that his adult accessory had a suction cup at the base of it. After putting on roughly about 10 pairs of gloves, it ended up stuck to his windshield!

RECOVER THE EVIDENCE NEW GUY

We were dispatched to the report of a man "playing with himself in a window." Upon our arrival, the caller quite *clearly* described the man, his "member", and his actions. We spoke with the man, who denied any misconduct, but a small trash can and abundance of facial tissue in and around it told a different story. My FTO, in his dry humor, initially tried to tell me to "recover the evidence." Thankfully, some other officers spared me this embarrassment. I also never bought fruit from the local grocery store that guy worked at ever again.

I'M BEAUTIFUL

We were dispatched to a local "high end" motel on the report of a robbery at one of the rooms. We arrived to find the victim quite ready to tell her story. Only the "her" was actually a **him**. "Pat" as I will call him, recounted how the stranger he had in his room had just absconded with his purse and money.

When asked how the stranger had come to be in the same room, Pat told us how the stranger had told Pat that he was "his deepest darkest fantasy."

Me: "Don't you find this type of behavior odd?"
Pat: (offended that I may be referring to his status as a transvestite) "What do you *mean?*"
Me: Inviting random strangers into your motel room because they told you they have a deep dark fantasy about you.
Pat: But . . . he had beer.
Me: That's how people get killed, Pat.
Pat: Not me honey, because I'm BEAUTIFUL. Now, you on the other hand, even if you put a wig on, you'd be the kind of person they'd want to hurt.
Me: Here's your report #.

BUT OLD PEOPLE LOVE CATS?

City X cars can you start heading to XX Main St. Caller states their elderly neighbor is holding their cat hostage . . .

MORE THAN THE MISSING SOCK

Cars, can you start heading to XX Main St. Caller states that there is a possible overdose in the basement laundry room. Victim may be IN the dryer.

I'M A WAITRESS

I was called to a domestic disturbance where the neighbors could hear a male and female arguing and throwing things in the living room. Showing up to the strong smell of marijuana, I knocked at the door as I saw the couple cleaning up their "supplies" through the front window.

The female answered the door, out of breath from running around hiding her treasure.

Me: Is everything ok?
Her: Yeah, fine, why?
Me: Well you're out of breath, were you working out?
Her: Yeah, I'm a waitress, I always work out
Me (thinking to self): wow... smoke some more.

SOMETHING BIT ME

I was once dispatched to a disturbance during an attempt at a vehicle repossession. I arrived to find the driver had tried to hook up the target car, but the owner jumped in the cab of his truck, took his keys from the ignition and in an epic battle over the keys, she bit him in the leg.

SEEMS LIKE THEY CAN CLEAN UP THEIR OWN MESS

City cars, start heading to 123 Main St. Mother has a broom, Son has a mop, and they're going at it pretty good.

I'M ONE OF YOU

We arrested a drunk fan at a kids' hockey game for disorderly conduct and subsequently resisting arrest. While in booking:

Him: C'mon guys, I'm one of you!
Me: What do you mean you're one of us?
Him: We're on the same side!
Me: What are you talking about?

Him: You know, doctors and cops, we support each other.
Me: You're a doctor? Of what?
Him: Horses.
Me: So you're a veterinarian?
Him: Yeah, whatever you call it.
Me: . . .

BUT I'M ONLY 18!

Bad guy: What am I being charged with?
Officer: A felony . . .
Bad guy: You can't charge me with a felony, I'm only 18!!
Officer: . . . .

YOU SHOULD RENAME YOUR NOTEBOOK

I was working a highway in northern Arizona not long after completing FTO, but still on probation. I spotted two vehicles traveling 90+ MPH and the front vehicle did not have a visible license plate. I caught up to both cars and attempted to stop the first one by splitting them. Fortunately, the second vehicle also stopped. I contacted the lead driver and asked where he was going. He stated Arizona. After I congratulated him for making it here, I asked him specifically where he was going. Scottsdale was his answer, but he could not provide anything further. I asked if he knew anyone in the other vehicle, and he stated that he did not. After getting his information I then contacted the other vehicle.

I asked the female her travel plans. She also stated Arizona, but she could not provide me with anything further. I asked if she knew the other driver. She identified him as "Slim" and showed me her tattoo of her boyfriend's name on her wrist. Even better, she stated she was driving his vehicle. She did not know where she was going, only that she was following him from Vegas to find work.

I conducted standard field sobriety tasks on him and hooked him for drunk driving. She was also ultimately hooked for, yup, drunk driving. Now I had two vehicles with two arrests and I just started to pull that string. During an inventory of the vehicle I located cash, large quantities of cocaine, marijuana, and methamphetamine. I located multiple identification cards for both suspects as well as multiple throw away phones. I was new on the road, but I knew I hit a treasure trove when I located a notebook entitled, *Businesses Used to Wash Money*. Page 1 was dedicated to a prostitution ring whose leader outlined his business expenses for his girls over 6 cities including Scottsdale. It was starting to come together.

In the rear seat I located court documents citing the male as the suspect of a prostitution sting in Iowa with the female suspect as the juvenile victim in that case. In her vehicle I located numerous sexual items including clothing, toys, and movies. She eventually admitted that she was following Slim to set up shop in Scottsdale.

His brand new Mercedes was seized and they were both arrested. The best part that sealed the deal for him as a sex and drug trafficker was the tattoo visible on his forearm - a picture of his girlfriend in a compromising position with the caption, "I Get Cash from a Ho's Ass". He took a plea for 2.5 years and then got sent back to Iowa for the remainder of his case that he was running from.

After that case I was given the nickname "Shit Magnet" and it is a patch that I wear proudly. I am proud to say that years later, I can still live up to my name.

SHE GOT TO LIKING IT

In 2009, my first year at my PD, and second year as a full time officer, during field training, I responded to a domestic disturbance at one of our trailer parks. Upon arrival, I was met at the door by a large lady with smeared makeup, dark red lipstick, messy black dyed and patchy hair, with one of those long cigarettes hanging from her mouth. Her voice was hoarse and she was dripping with sweat from her face. She invited us in, asking what the problem was. We informed her of the disturbance complaint and asked if there was a problem. She didn't say yes or no, but said we should go talk to "her man" in the back room. Still not sure what we were getting into, our backup officer stood with her and my FTO and I went to the back of the trailer. We met the other half, who was laying completely naked with a top sheet covering himself. We advised him of the complaint, after which he pointed to a jar of Vaseline next to the mattress, which also contained a slimy dildo. He then said they were just making love and "she got to liking it real good."

I BETTER FOLLOW THIS GUY

I was the "officer in charge" for a weekend one fall. The chief and our sergeants at the small department I worked for were all out of town. What an honor it was to be in charge. I was pretty excited. It was early morning and I was "monitoring traffic" on our main thoroughfare, sipping coffee and listening to AM radio to catch up on politics. I was watching cars quietly drive by and folks pulling in and out of the shopping plaza that I was sitting in. I watched as a healthy 6-point buck ran crazily across the main street, tongue hanging out and bloodied. As he began to approach a strip plaza, he was freaking out seeing his reflection in the windows and began to bang his antlers on the windows of the various stores. "I better follow this guy," I said to myself and slowly began to follow him in my car. He then ran to a neighboring building - a 4-story dental building with all glass windows. He stopped, stared, dipped his head and proceeded to run through the first floor windows and into the office. I threw my car into park and called out "I'll be out at XYZ for a buck in an occupied structure." I drew my gun and went on through the same window the buck entered through. There was broken glass, blood, fur and papers scattered everywhere. I began yelling "Police! There's a buck in here! Vacate immediately!" There was no response and no signs of anyone. I heard huffing from the deer in an adjacent room. I entered cautiously. When I located the deer, he looked at me, wild eyed, dipped his head, and ran at me. I fired one shot, hit him in the leg, he dropped, jumped back up and exited out another window, limping off into the woods behind the dental office. I immediately notified my sergeant who was away at a funeral. He arrived on scene an hour later, shaking his head and laughing. "Only you," he said. We never located the deer. The office building was occupied, but only in the floors above the incident and the owner of the building was thankful that he wasn't there when his office was taken over by a crazed buck in rut.

STOP THAT MAN

The tone goes out and dispatch says those famous words: "Units standby to copy" and for a moment everyone holds their breath.

"211 (robbery) just occurred at the Apple Store. Negative weapons will be strong arm. Repeat: 211 strong arm from the Apple Store. Suspect described as a WMA (white male adult) 5'10" about 170 lbs., grey hair, about . . . *uncomfortable pause before continuing in a more confused tone of voice* . . . suspect described as about 85-90 years old. Repeat, 85-90 years old. Last seen eastbound from the store on foot . . . *another uncomfortable pause before continuing in an almost laughing tone* . . . suspect last seen on foot eastbound from the store with his walker. *then actually laughing dispatch continues* RP (reporting party) advises he is in foot pursuit of the suspect."

I CALLED YOU BECAUSE I HATE YOU

My partner and I got dispatched to a disturbance between a mother and her 31-year-old son. We arrived on scene and knocked on the door. The mother answered the door and promptly told us that we need to remove her son from the house.

I ask, "What seems to be the problem?"
Mother: "He is lazy and doesn't do anything around the house."
Me: "Ma'am, does your son live here?"
Mother: "Yes, but I don't have time for him. I got bills to pay and he doesn't help me out."

Me: "Ma'am, that is not reason enough for me to remove your son from the location. You will have to have him legally evicted."

Mother: "You don't have the right to tell me who I can and can't have in my house."

Me: "Ma'am, I'm pretty sure that is why you called for police."

WRONG BUILDING. VERY WRONG.

We were at a cockroach infested apartment complex looking to make contact with a suicidal male. Of course he wouldn't answer, and neither would the other 6 rooms as there was a camera at the front door. We noticed a few lights on upstairs, so we tried in vain to get someone at the door. I finally took my flashlight and shined it through the ground floor apartment window and what do I see burning my retina but a fat ol' guy sitting at his computer in mid-stroke, and the light didn't even phase him. I averted my eyes quickly only to find his ol' lady sitting on the couch two feet away watching TV as if her man isn't sitting their slapping himself. A few more kicks at the door and their apartment door flew open and out stormed the lady. She was yelling, upset that we ruined her man's evening, I guess. Once I composed myself and got ready to enter, I noticed the man in the doorway pulling up his tightie-whities (in need of a new pair I might add) and trying to pull his shorts up. I could hardly walk to the patrol car because of how hard we were laughing. My partner then informed me we were at the wrong building.

HURRY UP, HE HAS A CHAINSAW

Dispatch came on saying we needed to head to a residence. The son was reporting that his father and a neighbor were going at it, and that his father came home grabbed the chainsaw and was heading over to deal with the neighbor. We arrived and found that the father and neighbor were "going at it" by simply trying to make a purchase deal over the chainsaw. The father ended up selling it for $100.00. The neighbor was satisfied, and felt it was a good deal. The son got a blast for being a dumbass and calling 911.

THE STARFISH LADY

We live in a small rural town in central Minnesota. My husband works for the city police department, which consists of 6 officers, but we are the county seat so the deputies, state patrolmen, and city PD basically function as one force for the area. They have a traveling trophy called the "*horse's ass award*" which is given to the officer who makes the funniest "oops" every year. A few years ago, one of the city officers received the award for the following situation:

He arrested a drunk woman who was being disorderly and violent. As they got to the jail, she refused to get out of the back of the squad car. As he tried to coerce her out, she laid on her back and started kicking and thrashing at him. Finally, he grabbed hold of her legs in order to pull her to the edge of the vehicle and remove her from the squad. As he pulled, her prosthetic leg came off in his hand! It took him a few seconds to realize he didn't just pull her actual leg off. The moment was priceless as he stood there shocked and horrified, holding this woman's leg while she's still screaming at him from inside the squad. Not only did he win the award that year, but would probably be in the running for the "horse's ass" lifetime award.

NOTHING LIKE A BRAND NEW PATROL CAR

I started the graveyard shift in a brand new car, just rolled off the yard after getting the light bar, radio and siren installed, with just 100 miles on it. The boys and I met for coffee after briefing, and as I was getting into my brand new cruiser, I told my partners, "I am gonna get in a pursuit and see what this thing can do." Not 5 minutes later I saw a car swerving in its lane, so I activated the lights and called out a T-stop. The guy kept going, and I thought, "no way." Yup, he kept going. Siren on, but he kept going. I called out the pursuit, and off we went. I am now out of the city, still chasing with lights and sirens, and here come the troops. During the pursuit I called out the regular stuff like conditions and speed. The funny thing is the guy never went over the speed limit.

By the time I reached the next city 10 minutes later, a road block had been set up by the county guys and the driver finally yielded. Since we were doing a felony stop, my brother-in-law who works as a sheriff was standing on my passenger side door with his gun out. As I was giving the driver orders, the driver yelled, "your lights are not on!" My brother-in-law looked over at the top of my cruiser and said "your lights are not on." I looked and, sure enough, my light bar was dark. I looked inside and my light switch was flashing green, meaning my light bar was supposedly on. My corner marker strobes were on, my headlights were flashing high to low, but my light bar was not on, which explained why I could see flashing lights in front of me while chasing this guy. We dusted the guy off and he was not drunk, just tired. He said, "I saw your headlights and strobe lights on the front of your car but not red or blue lights so I didn't think you were really a cop." By this time there were about 10 cops on the scene, and I turned around to see all 10 standing about 50 yards away from me laughing, while I stood alone and tried to explain the situation to this poor motorist.

Oh, but the night's not over. I headed back to the barn, downed the car and checked out another unit. As I left the office I saw another speeding car. I lit up the car, crested a hill, and immediately hit a large construction barrier in the middle of the road, ripping off the driver's side mirror of the second cruiser I had just checked out not 5 minutes before. I returned to the office, walked into the sergeant's office with the mirror in my hand. Smiling, he said, "You're done. Check out a bicycle, or walk the rest of your shift.

I came to work the next night, and the station looked weirdly empty. I walked into the locker room where it was dark, but I could see lights way back near my locker. I found that my buddies had wired a light bar - a full decommissioned light bar - to my locker and it was on and running. To top it off, everyone came in to give me a shitty golf clap. Yeah, this really happened. Who had the worst night ever? This guy!

VALENTINE'S DAY CAME EARLY

I was en route to a domestic in progress when dispatch advised the male was armed with a bow. I showed up on scene and parked about 40 yards from the apartment building. As I exited my patrol car I saw a grown man step out onto a third floor balcony wearing a giant diaper with duct tape securing it in place. He was holding a bow with an arrow knocked. I yelled for him to drop the bow. Come to find out the ass clown was off his meds, and actually thought he was Cupid spreading love. The bow was a child's toy (looked real from 40 yards and 3 stories). The arrows were little sticks with fake Indian arrowheads duct taped on.

GOATED INTO A REPORT

I responded to a call about a goat loose near the post office in one of the communities we serve. The goat was head-butting customers as they exited the building. I showed up and this goat was wandering around the parking lot while a bunch of people were pressed up against the inside of the post office door, afraid to come out. So I got out of my car and talked to one of the local residents, who told me the goat had already clobbered one poor guy and wouldn't let anyone out of the building. At that moment the goat approached me and reared up on its hind legs. I'm 6'1" and this goat was a head taller than me when up on its hind legs. It came up to me and cocked its head, ready to smash me. Not having anywhere to go, I punched it in the face. Needless to say, it didn't exactly have much of an effect. So I drew my Taser X26 and "let two fly." The goat gave a long and loud bleat as it fell face first onto the pavement with its hind legs still locked out, like a furry, horned tripod. It stayed that way for the whole five seconds. Once the ride was over it jumped up and scampered back home. When I got back to the office I, of course, drew up a proper Taser use report form and turned it into my sergeant.

BUT I STOPPED...SORTA

While parked on the street watching a stop sign, a vehicle came and completely blew through the sign. Halfway through the intersection, the driver saw me, slammed on the brakes, and stopped in the middle of the intersection. Then, the driver put the car in reverse, backed up to before the stop sign, stopped, then continued properly through the intersection. I was laughing and had planned to let him go with a warning, but unfortunately he was in violation of his restricted license. Made my day though.

WELL THAT WAS EASY

One night I stopped a guy for speeding and crossing a double yellow line.
Me: "Do you know why I stopped you?"
Him: "Yes."
Me (after a long pause): "Why is that?"
Him (with slow, slurred speech): "Because I had too much to drink and I'm not safe to drive."

BABIES 'R' US

I once got a non-emergency call from a woman looking for advice:
Caller: "Hi, I'm three months pregnant and I have a problem."
Me: "Ok, do you need an ambulance?"
Caller: "Oh no, I'm trying to figure out the father of the baby."
Me: "Um, I don't know that I can help you there . . ."
Caller: "Well, just listen. I have only been - you know, intimate - with this one guy for the past year, but I hooked up with another guy before him. Could my baby be from that other guy?"
Me: "You haven't been intimate with anyone else for the past year?"

Caller: "No."

Me, trying to keep as calm and non-sarcastic as possible: "Well, ma'am, the baby is your boyfriend's since pregnancies last nine months and you've been with him longer than that."

Caller, sounding sincerely relieved: "Oh, thank goodness. Now where can I get help with baby clothes and that sort of thing?"

I directed her to the right people to call and then busted a gut laughing!

THE COURTESY FLUSH

Every Cop knows that the most truly difficult part of the day is trying to use the facilities with all that gear. Officer Smith would agree*

While working in a plainclothes unit, Officer Smith (name changed to protect his identity) had to answer the call of nature with a #2. So he picked a stall, dropped trow, and started his business. Now he is on duty, and has his gun and other gear on his belt. As you can imagine, this weighs things down a bit, but since this is the office washroom and it's clean, he just lets the weight drag his gear and pants to the floor.

Well, it turns out that this was an exceptional #2 with an exceptional stink. So, being the courteous guy that he is, Smith decided to do a courtesy flush to get rid of some of the smell, but before he's finished his business. However, this was an exceptional poop and wasn't going down without a fight. Or more aptly described, a clog.

So that's when the toilet decided to overflow. Over the edge comes all Smith's dirty business and onto the floor, soaking his pants and gun and all his other gear.

So, after taking a few minutes to run to the sink and try to clean his clothes and gear as best he can, poor Smith had to take a walk of shame back to his desk to get his keys and inform his colleague that he was going home early to change and get cleaned up, and that there was a slight mess in the 3rd floor washroom.

WHO CAN RESIST LEMON DROPS

How about the time I was dispatched to deal with a 50-pound or so pot belly pig wandering in an intersection in town at 8 a.m. on a Sunday morning. I was a rookie and when the call went out I thought it was a prank but sure enough it wasn't. I ended up using the only thing I had in my bag, sugar free lemon drops, to bribe the pig to the sidewalk and then kept giving them to the pig and trying to keep it out of traffic and safe for 30 minutes until animal control was able to get there. Then when he got there with the dog cage it was comical watching the 2 of us try to get the pig into the cage! As anyone who has ever dealt with a pot belly pig knows, getting a leash on one - much less getting in a cage - isn't easy (especially when it weighs 50 pounds, the noises it makes sound like you are harming it, and so on). I even have a picture of the pig saved somewhere around here . . .

SIZE SOMETIMES MATTERS

So, there I was, a trooper in Colorado for all of 18 months, and I loved my campaign hat. One day we were stopping traffic for a wide load. This thing was a rather large blade for a power generating windmill, and the road has a series of switchbacks, so it would have taken both lanes going up the hill. I had traffic stopped, campaign hat on, and I was letting people know it would be a five-minute delay for the wide load. I walked up to this lifted diesel truck, my chin coming up to the bottom of the window (I am a 5'10" female). I advised the skinhead-hard-looking dude driving that a wide load was coming and that he would have to wait a couple of minutes. He asked if he needed to move over to the shoulder to allow it to pass. My response: "It is more about the length than the width." Now this little 18-month trooper, trying to look like a badass in her campaign hat, is turning all shades of red and said skinhead-hard-looking dude has a smug look on his face as I walk away. I wish I made that up . . .

WHAT BABY?

We use to have this "S24" in our jurisdiction: that's someone with some sort of mental instability in our area. She used to always call 911 every single day and night regarding some outlandish story about someone blowing black smoke in her face and taking her baby, or the president coming over to her house and kidnapping her. Usually these calls were reserved for the rookies to handle when they were on FTO. One night she called and asked for police and fire to respond due to a medical call. Of course, we arrived first and she was outside screaming and yelling her usual about someone taking her baby. The fire department showed up, pulled up into her yard and driveway and they all bailed out and started their approach. She started screaming, "You just ran over my baby, you just ran over my baby!" The fire personnel freaked out and started running all over the place looking and then backed the engine up, jumped and continued their frantic search! Of course we were all laughing hysterically watching as they were freaking out! Finally, they saw us and stopped, realizing that there was no baby, and looking at us with that look of throwing daggers our way! It was so funny! Needless to say, from that point on they always responded to her calls but took her demands with a little more observation!

DROP THE JAR SIR

On patrol, I noticed a car under a street light in a city park that closed at 10 p.m., so I went to check it out. The road was cobble stone, so I had to forget stealth mode. Anyway, I pulled up behind the guy and spot-lighted him. As I approached, I saw the driver's side window down and say "Sir, put your hands up where I can see them." No response.

"Oh crap!" comes to mind. I continued on, with weapon ready. "Sir!" I yelled; still nothing. I got to the window, shined my light on him and he was steadily "going at it" . . . in a mayonnaise jar! I didn't know whether to be angry or to laugh.

Again I said "Sir!" He was totally in the home stretch, so I just kind of stood by and waited. Finally, "Houston, we have touchdown." He ever so calmly screwed the lid on the jar of mayo and then and only then appeared to notice me. He jumped; I was laughing. I said, "Sir I don't have to ask what you were doing, but why here in a closed park under a street light? His response was that his wife was mad at him, refused him any assistance, and told him if he wanted it, he'd have to do it himself! Well, obviously he did! The mayo jar was to take back to his wife to show her he took her comment literally. And as Paul Harvey would say: now you know the rest of the story!

I'M SORRY CAN YOU REPEAT

I met my husband in the mall parking lot to give him the clothes that I had in the trunk of the patrol car so he could take them to the dry cleaners (I know, I know, but . . .). While reaching for the final few items, I said "Love you, too. Everything goes but the bra." However, I had keyed the mic when I reached in!

Clicks all over the City! And there ya go.

HOW WE ROLL IN CANADA

Well, what do you do when a 154-pound sheep is running loose in traffic? Well in Canada, you get a mountie and a couple other cops to chase it around a while, drive alongside of it, hit it with a Taser, then sit on it and pose for pictures that make it all the way to national headquarters . . . but not before it was already published in the news. The officers literally had to sit on the sheep until animal control arrived as it was "still squirming around."

EVEN JESUS LIKES SNACKS

My partner and I had just walked into a local convenience store for a quick drink and snack when the shift Lieutenant radioed that he had a suspicious subject that just resisted him and fled from a stop he was making. Of course, we dropped everything, blasted a couple of miles down the road and set up a quick perimeter. The "bad guy" was located in a back yard and subsequently bitten by the K9 officer so that he finally was "persuaded" to surrender.

A couple of us brought him out to the front curb to meet the medics. I sat him down against a car. While we were letting the adrenalin settle, I told this dude, "Man you ruined my snack."

In a very dramatic and dejected tone he replied, "Why would you say that? *What would Jesus say?*"

The officer standing on the other side of him said, "Dude, you're talking to the Chaplain."

Now the bad guy looked at me and asked, "You're the Chaplain?"
Me: "Yep. And I think Jesus would say you ruined my snack."

Another successful chaplain consult complete.

THE NO REPORT ROBBERY SPECIAL

I only needed to clear this call with the following notes:

"Report of robbery on Skytrain. Complainant states she paid $20 for crack but dealer took money and only gave her $10 worth of crack. Crack was consumed prior to police arrival. I advised Complainant that she received the product, so it was not theft or robbery. If she was unhappy with the product, she could go to small claims court. Civil issue. File Concluded. No Further Action Required."

A GNINRAW

My hubby confirmed a woman was speeding on radar. He walked up to the driver's side window and started his usual spiel: "Good morning. My name is Officer Smith. Is there some reason you were doing 53 in the 35 mph zone?"

She looked up at him and quickly answered, "I'm dyslexic?" He let her go with a warning before he started laughing.

WHAT KIND OF STRAW IS THIS?

On one particular drunk driving stop, the offender was so inebriated, he had no idea he was speaking to a police officer. When I tried to administer the breathalyzer, the idiot sucked on the device instead of blowing, and complained *"There's nothing coming through the straw, dude."*

THE MOST CONSIDERATE CAR THIEF

I received a call from a frantic victim stating that someone had stolen his vehicle from his driveway. I arrived on scene and made contact with a guy that seemed beside himself. He went on to explain that when he woke up this morning, he noticed that his car had been stolen and subsequently replaced with the same make/model/color vehicle.

He further stated that the thief even took the time to change all of the locks in the vehicle so that all of his keys still work, including his ignition key. They then replaced the license plates with ones that are registered to him. I asked him if he was sure that the car in the driveway wasn't his car and he was adamant that it wasn't. I ran the plate and verified that the VIN matched. This guy wouldn't hear anything I had to say about it and I eventually told him that I would write a report and find his vehicle. He was satisfied with that. "I'll be 10-8, dispatch, subject is Code 13. No report."

I laughed for a good two days.

WHAT'S YOUR LOCATION?

I had a partner that called out in pursuit. When asked his location, he responded "I'm right behind him!"

WHAT HAS BEEN SEEN CANNOT BE UNSEEN

While my husband was still on FTO (on the job training) he was called to a domestic dispute. His training officer knew the address they were going to and asked him to clear the house. As he cleared each room and entered the bedroom, he found the caller, a very obese elderly man, on top of the bed *naked on all fours.* The worst part was that he was facing away from the doorway. My husband turned around to find his training officer trying hard to contain his laughter.

FORGETFUL COPS AND ROBBERS

We were dispatched to an apartment for a citizen assist. Dispatch simply advised us to "Check the notes" with a hint of laughter. We arrived to use our handcuff keys to release a wife whose husband was so eager to play his part that he forgot he would need a handcuff key at some point.

CAKE NAZI

I responded to a burglary call and entered the apartment to find the suspect inside trying to eat a handful of chocolate cake. I told her that she was under arrest, and she asked if she could at least finish the cake. In my best Seinfeld "Soup Nazi" voice, I knocked the cake out of her hand and yelled, "*No cake for you!*"

THE HOBBIT FIGHT

I was a new guy with about five months on the job, fresh off FTO. I was working dayshift and got called in by the lieutenant to speak with a female in the lobby. At the time, I felt like I could handle anything, probably due in part to my naiveté.

When I walked into the lobby, I knew I was in for more than I bargained for. To say she was heavyset was putting it mildly; she was also barefoot. Her feet looked like she had left the Shire and she never returned. They were pitch black and her toenails were deemed dangerous weapons, probably banned in several states.

Upon speaking with this woman, I quickly realized two things: First, I must have done something to piss off the lieutenant, and second, her feet were illustrative of her unbalanced state of mind. I waited to let this woman know she was going to be committed until the EMS cot arrived. When the cot arrived, the fight was on, and she did not disappoint. It took six officers and the chief of police to escort this woman to the cot. Being the new guy, I had the legs.

While I was attempting to strap her lower extremities to the cot, she was able to writhe free, kicking me in the mouth. And by kicking, I mean raking her 80 grit big toe, raptor claw and all, along the inside of my bottom lip. In doing so, she not only took the fight out of me, but me out of the fight. I was bested.

Fearing what undiscovered diseases her foot (petri-dish) contained, I refrained from swallowing the unsavory flavor in my mouth. I made it to the back of the station where I not only spit out what was in my mouth, but the contents of my lunch as well. The moral of the story is don't get caught puking by another officer; you will never live it down.

X-FILES

My partner and I were dispatched to a disturbance call, and of course it was right near the end of my shift, so my enthusiasm level was less than high. According to the call there was a male and a female in some sort of argument.

When I got on my computer and read it, I recognized the subjects as a couple of regulars. The guy was an old drunk guy and the girl a bit younger with a history of mental health issues. They had an on again, off again relationship which allowed her to stay in the apartment, although he spent most nights on the couch because he really couldn't deal with her.

We arrived at the apartment and I contacted the male (let's call him Fred). Fred was in a bit of a stupor and told me he was arguing with (let's call her Ethel) about rent money. I stayed in the living room with Fred while my partner went towards the back bedroom to talk with Ethel. The first thing I heard as my partner got to the threshold of the bedroom was "Awwww geez, can you put some clothes on?"

A few moments later Ethel emerged from the bedroom wearing a just long enough t-shirt. She was standing in the poorly-lit kitchen talking to my partner. Ethel claimed the argument was over a plethora of issues. Knowing the subjects and being near the end of our shift we told him to work it out in the morning and go to sleep, to which Ethel immediately piped up: "But he raped me!"

My partner took a sharp breath, looked at Ethel and said, "No, he didn't."

"Yes, he did!" replied Ethel. "He did and it made me have a miscarriage."

"I didn't touch you," burbled Fred from the couch.

"I think you are confused," my partner said, looking at the ground. He turned his head slightly and looked at Ethel's feet. He turned on his flashlight and asked "Is that blood on your feet?"

Ethel looked down at her feet and said "Yes that's from when he raped me and I had a miscarriage. But it's okay, I saved the baby; it's in the pool. I put it in the pool so it would live. It's there right now"

My partner looked at me with a blank stare as I stared back, equally blank.

"In the pool right here at the apartment?" I asked

"Yes" replied Ethel "We need to help it; I put it there so it would be okay"

"Can you show me?" I asked.

"Yes, follow me."

My partner and I followed Ethel to the pool at the center of the apartment complex. The whole area was dark and poorly lit.

"Right there in the pool" Ethel exclaimed, "I put it in the pool right there."

I leaned as far over the low fence surrounding the pool as I could, straining to look into the pool.

"You see anything?" my partner asked.

"I think there is something in there," I said, waiting for my partner to volunteer to go over the fence. Reading his face, I clamored over the fence and slowly walked up to the side of the pool.

"Crap!" I said.

"What is it?" asked my partner.

"There's something in the pool," I said.

"No there's not," he replied.

"I'm afraid there is." I peered over the edge of the pool and in the shadows I could see a shape - a lump really. A lump which at a profile appeared consistent with something in a fetal position. It looked far too big to be a premature baby, but the shape was unmistakable with the exception of the head--which was oddly shaped.

"What is it?" asked my partner

"It's my *BABY!*" screamed Ethel.

"It looks like a baby," I said.

"No it's not" he said.

"Maybe. I can't really tell."

I walked over to the fence to find a net, but all I could find was a rescue hook. I took the hook off the fence and walked back to the pool edge.

"Okay," I began. "I'm going to try to see what this is, but I want to warn you if it is a baby I may vomit in the pool."

Gently I eased the pole down into the water. The width of the hook created a wake in the water and the little object rocked gently back and forth. I was certain it was a baby; I could see the arms and legs tucked up into the torso. I tried to roll it over but just couldn't get it to move the way I wanted.

"What is it?" my partner asked.

"I'm not sure."

"IT'S MY BABY!!" screamed Ethel.

I continued to work the hook near the object, which in one sudden movement rolled onto its back. Staring back at me were two large oversized almond shaped green eyes. It was a fetus alright: a plastic, alien fetus.

"It's a frigging doll," I said in relief. "An alien doll."

"NO IT'S NOT," screamed Ethel. "IT'S NOT A DOLL, IT'S MY BABY!"

"It's a doll," I assured my partner who turned to the now hysterical Ethel and said,

"It's not a baby, it's a doll."

"Are you sure?" asked Ethel.

"Yes I'm sure, it's not your baby," said my partner (using his best Jedi voice).

"Oh, okay" she said "But what about the miscarriage?"

"You didn't have one."

"I didn't?"

"No."

"So I didn't get raped?" Ethel said in confusion.

"No you didn't," continued my Jedi partner.

"Oh," said Ethel. "I guess I just spilled juice on my feet."

"You should take your meds and go to bed," said my partner.

"Yes, I need to take my meds and go to bed," repeated Ethel.

She turned and walked back to the apartment and took her meds. Fred was snoring on the couch. My partner and I walked back to our patrol car with a feeling of relief and disbelief. Ethel is still a semi-regular caller, and she recently told me she was Princess Di.

THE TURKEY WAS THAT GOOD

Once upon a Thanksgiving circa 1985, I responded to a rescue call of a man with a hand injury. I arrived and made contact with the reporting party. He had a giant carving fork impaled in the back of his left hand. He and dad were arguing about who got the leftover turkey leg when Junior decided to grab it and never let go. So, like any normal dad, this one stabbed his son with the carving fork and was gnawing on the tasty turkey leg! Dad was triumphant that he won, and yet puzzled as to why he was going to jail and his son going to the hospital. The case never went to court and that was the one and only time I've ever responded to that address. Wacky family.

I'D RATHER HAVE THE COMPLAINT

My partner and I arrested a couple for domestic violence. We couldn't determine the primary aggressor, so we took them both. The female has a baby daddy who is a corporal at the local sheriff's office, and she is a frequent flyer for us (always causing a problem). She thought only the boyfriend was going to jail, and she was pissed to find out otherwise. She filed a complaint on me saying that I was rude, inconsiderate, and I lied. A couple days later, my partner got a 'thank you' note from her for his professionalism and courtesy, and apologizing if her complaint on me got him in trouble. A week later he walked out the door of his house to walk his K9 Bronson and he found a 4-page love letter on his patrol car pronouncing her love for my partner, providing her phone number, and saying he "can come over any time he wants."

I died laughing when he texted me and told me.

IT'S NOT LIKE IT'S BRAIN SURGERY

My dad was a cop in New Jersey for 24 years and where he worked, a particular underpass would always flood badly. As a senior patrolman, his job was to stand by to assist in rescue efforts during the heavy rains, because someone was bound to create or find themselves in an emergency.

One particular evening, under heavy rains, the underpass flooded as usual. My father, sitting at the top, noticed a white Volkswagen approaching that showed no signs of trying to stop. The lights on the patrol car were on and he let the sirens wail and was yelling on the PA: "Stop, the water is too deep!"

As my cop dad is shaking his head, he yelled at the driver, now stalled and stuck in 4 feet of water, "What are you doing!?" From the roof of his car the man yelled "I'm a neurosurgeon and I have to get to the hospital!" Ever with the quick wit, my dad retorted "I pray you never operate on my brain because you have no common sense."

That day, I came home from cheerleading practice and will always remember how hard my father was laughing. When I asked him why, he said, "Sit down, we need to have a talk about common sense."

THE SCREAMING TREE

While working the night shift I got a call from dispatch just before sunrise for the report of a "screaming tree" which was called in by an elderly female. It wasn't even my district, but my smartass older brother was working as a dispatcher and thought it'd be funny to send me to the crazy lady call.

I arrived with my partner and another officer plus our bored sergeant. Expecting to have a crazy or drunk reporting party, she answered the door and said, "It's still screaming, want to go see?"

We get into the back yard and sure as hell there came a shrill screeching sound from about 20' up an old fir tree. Upon further inspection I saw the source: A presumably rabid raccoon perched on a branch and clearly not happy. I turned to comment to my buddy and sarge, but found they had both retreated in fear about 25 yards away. As luck would have it the rabid raccoon was unstable and started to fall, but caught itself by clamping its jaws on a branch about 10' off the ground and continued to scream.

New problem: It was now on the other side of the fence, near a main street and directly along the path of school children who would soon be walking by on the way to school. Animal control would take too long to arrive so we went around the back fence and I decided to put a 9mm round into the screamer. The animal fell to the ground and went silent. Problem solved; that is until I shined my light in its face to confirm. Without warning, Lazarus the screaming raccoon "came to life" again and screamed at me.

Startled, I jumped, (honestly, I think I started screaming myself) and quickly fired a second round. The animal fell silent again. This had to be it. Well, it was . . . until my light hit its face again and like some type of alien, it opened its eyes and started screeching at me again, causing another 9mm discharge and still more shrieking from me. The evil beast was slain for certain on that, my third attempt to eliminate it. Unless it's buried somewhere awaiting another resurrection.

YO QUIERO BOND MONEY

While working intake years ago, an officer brought in a man who claimed, "No hablo inglés." So the cop asked out loud if any of the deputies at intake spoke Spanish.

My husband, very seriously, shouts out "I do," and marches over to the perp to play interpreter. Looking the man deep in his eyes, he says "Yo quiero Taco Bell," and everyone started laughing. Then, my husband says, "No, seriously though, I don't speak Spanish, but it looks like this guy had $500 on him that's going to disappear."

Out of nowhere, the guy, who "doesn't speak English" shouts out, "Hey, that's my money! You can't do that!"

My husband turns to the guy with a shit eating grin on his face and says, "Gotcha!" The bad guy smiled sheepishly and started laughing, then everyone within earshot started laughing, too.

A DEAL'S A DEAL

I may not be an officer but my LEO came home one day and told me he had gone to an older lady's trailer who calls quite often. This particular time she was said to be having an argument with her male neighbor. My husband asked her if she knew this man well and if there had been any relations. She shook her head and said no. Then after a few moments she said "Wait! I did f--- him for a turkey once."

IT'S NOT WHAT IT LOOKS LIKE

What started out as a fairly straight forward driving on a suspended license arrest quickly turned into a handcuffed guy who began to resist my efforts to search and get him in the back of the car. As I finally began to get him under control, my senior officer pulled up and started laughing at me. As I looked down, I understood why - the guy's pants were at his ankles and he was - yes, you guessed it - going commando. I'm assuming many people driving by got their laugh for the day.

THIS PLACE IS AWESOME

I clearly recall my first day on the job at my current department. It was the year 2000 and I walked in an hour early (still do today) to get ready for work.

I walked through the roll call room and saw my sergeant sitting at his desk. "Good morning, sir," I said politely. He looked up at me, took his glasses off and said, "You shut your f#$/!ing mouth, don't say a word the rest of the day." I walked to my locker and considered walking out and trying to get my job back at the smaller department I had come from in the Upper Peninsula of Michigan. But, I sucked it up, got changed and walked out into roll call. I met the crew and was assigned to my Field Training Officer.

We hit the streets and started our 8-hour shift. We were about three hours in when we received a report of a suspect that did a "smash and grab" of a liquor store and was now walking through one of our apartment complexes. We responded and sure enough, there he was in the parking lot. My FTO, for better or worse, said "I'm going to pull up next to him; you get out and grab him."

We pulled up and I jumped out as the bad guy looked at me and took off running. I reached out, grabbed him by his jacket, then he turned and punched me . . . right in the face. He even ripped my brand new crisp and clean uniform. I didn't let go, picked him up over my head and gently placed him on the ground where a huge mud puddle happened to be (of course). My FTO hopped out and we slapped the cuffs on. Then it was time for the fun stuff of report writing.

I'm now thinking this place is AWESOME! I went home after work, where I was staying with another officer and walked through the door looking like I was hit by a tornado. My roommate looks at me and said, "WTF happened to you?"

I said "This place is awesome!" Then we drank beer the rest of the night. LOL! The end.

NOT THE GOOD KIND OF NAKED EITHER

While I was in field training we received a call on a Sunday morning about a burglary in progress at an apartment. Upon arriving and speaking to the residents, they told us that they knew someone was in their apartment because the window was open and an unrecognized pair of shoes were still sitting in the front room. After backup arrived, we entered the apartment to clear it and find any suspects. About a minute later I heard, "Hey ROOK!" and I knew I was in for something.

I got to the back bedroom and my FTO told me, "We found the suspect; she is on the other side of that bed; go hook her up." I cautiously moved toward the other side because I got a hint something was up. I got to the other side of the bed and there she is in all of her drunken, go-into-the-wrong-apartment splendor; halfway under the bed and out like a light. Oh, did I mention she was topless? Not the good kind of topless but the sort of all things moving far south type of topless.

I hooked her up, and finally was able to wake her to get her out of the place. We grabbed her a shirt and she was adamant she is in her friend's apartment. According to the apartment renters, they'd never seen this lady. However, they were getting ready to move, so they had packed their pantry items into boxes. The drunk "burglar" had thought she was doing her friends a favor and unpacked the boxes and loaded the pantry before passing out naked in the bedroom . . .half under the bed.

EVERY FAMILY HAS THAT UNCLE

I recall a run from the mid 90's when I was working in Southwest Detroit. My partner and I were blessed to be working on Christmas day. We were dispatched to a domestic situation on a street, like many in the area, where only a few houses would have visible home addresses. So we arrived to the area and I was riding shotgun. My partner was vigilantly looking for an address when I saw where we should go and started laughing. I told my partner "I think I found it." Then he saw what I had observed: A fully decorated Christmas tree lying on the front lawn along with the entire Christmas dinner, all of which were thrown through the front picture window by the irate uncle who was now gone. Needless to say it was easy to find that call.

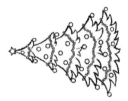

I DON'T THINK THAT'S COVERED

Quite a few years ago, my partner and I arrived to a domestic violence call to find an open front door. The husband was gone; the wife was gone. In fact, no one was home at all. It turns out that the husband left after an argument with his bat shit crazy wife. She left because he left. But before she left, she pulled the hose and lawn sprinkler into the living room and turned it on high. I doubt the home owner's insurance paid out.

SPIT SAUCE

I was sent to a Famous Dave's BBQ in response to a disorderly person on St. Patrick's day a few years ago. Once inside, a *robust* (or is it rotund) female decided that when I asked her to leave, it would be a good time to spray me with the "Devil Spit" sauce. The fight was on right there at the bar. I eventually took her to my patrol car and obviously to jail.

Once in the jail she refused to walk and I had to pull her by the legs into the detox cell. Suddenly, an overwhelmingly nauseating smell hit me at which time I looked down and this said female was literally shitting her pants as I watched, and shit the consistency of grease was leaking from her pant legs.

All you could see on our surveillance tape was me throwing up directly onto her like Jeff Goldblum in "The Fly." There she was in a pile of her own excrement and my vomit. So nasty.

WOULD YOU LIKE AN ALTOID, OFFICER?

One hot summer day I was taking a mentally unstable male to be petitioned at the hospital for evaluation. He whipped out an Altoids box and eagerly desired to show me the contents. Well, he had been collecting scabs for years and the box was filled with them. The smell of old scab in a hot house hit me...and *I fainted*.

IS THERE A PROBLEM OFFICER?

I was working midnights overtime on the freeway when I stopped a car and approached. Inside were two guys that couldn't care less that I was there and attempting to get their attention. I stood there in amazement as they continued giggling and pulling on each other's wieners.

SEE WHY I CAN'T WEAR THIS THING?

I was working a seat belt detail from a state grant and stopped a violator. I told him why I stopped him and he immediately began screaming "The fu$&ing thing chokes me, damn it, the fu$&ing seat belt chokes me!" As I stood there bewildered, he then wrapped the seat belt around his neck and began strangling himself. I was like, "Hey man, it's just a seat belt!" He kept going and the next thing you see is me pulling him out of the driver's side window and fighting with him in the middle of a busy intersection. Good times.

SAY MY NAME, SAY MY NAME

It was a warm summer evening in Indianapolis and in my area, it was more uncommon for someone to *have* a license on a traffic stop than otherwise. So, we came to loathe traffic enforcement due to the normal outcome of long waits for tow trucks and copious amounts of paperwork.

On this particular night I was in my usual hiding hole trying to scarf down some food. I saw a car coming down the lane that I was at the end of, easily doing 45 in a 25, so at that point I put down my sandwich and hit the lights. The car pulled over immediately and I went through the usual process of running the plate, and was pleased to see it appeared to at least be a valid plate.

I got out and approached the vehicle driver side and saw a woman that appeared to have forgotten her weave at home. I went through the "why I stopped you" routine and asked for her for her license and registration, which she immediately had ready.

I ended up writing her a warning and returned to her car to say, "Well Da-shia, I'm going to give you a warn-" which is when she scowled at me, stopping me mid-sentence, gazing at me as if I had a large booger hanging from my nose and indignantly said: "Honey, it's Da-DASH-ia, Da-Dash-ia. Da dash ain't silent!" (pause to read that again in case you missed it) I stood there dumbfounded until I couldn't resist cracking a large smile, handed her the documentation back and made my way back to my car before I made things worse.

DOWN ON THE GROUND! ALL OF YOU!

I believe it was a sunny spring morning working interdiction on Interstate 75, near the violent and drug-infested City of Detroit.

My partner, (aka "sizzle") was my jump man that day. We tried to settle in for a few minutes and get our eyes to focus on vehicles zipping by at 80 mph, no easy task. Finally, we saw a vehicle of interest, pulled out and got behind it and noted some pretty furtive gestures inside the vehicle.

Then, as if we wouldn't notice, the driver switched with the passenger, and the original driver somehow jumped in the back seat and laid down.

We were obviously on pretty high-alert, Starsky & Hutch style. We finally got the vehicle to come to a stop, and as we approached we ordered the female to keep her hands on the roof while trying to extract the male from the backseat.

The guy in the back seat began reaching toward his cargo pocket area, so we pulled harder. That's when BAM, he came out while dragging a full fake leg, as he was an amputee. Guns out, leg on the ground, one-legged man in cuffed right there on the side of the expressway.

Dispatch received calls from a few drivers passing by, reporting officers with their guns out and appearing to fight with someone and possibly in need of help. At the end of it all we brought shoeless/legless Joe Criminal to jail for whatever crime it was he was believed to have committed. We shared a few laughs and also received a swift talking to by the lieutenant for not relaying everything that was going on up on the interstate, but even he couldn't help but laugh at the experience.

LOOK AWAY KIDS, LOOK AWAY

While working midnights, sometime around 0530 hours, some

other officers and I were dispatched to an apartment on a report of an unknown person sleeping on the caller's couch. Once we arrived and entered the first floor hallway of the complex, we noticed a shoe and set of car keys sitting on the floor at the base of the stairs to the second floor. As we walked upstairs to the apartment we noticed a pair of pants, a wallet and a shoe that matched the same shoe at the base of the stairs on the floor outside of the caller's apartment. The caller told us that there was an unknown naked male sleeping on her couch and she had no idea who the male was. The caller proceeded to tell us that she possibly left her front door unlocked prior to going to bed earlier in the night. As we entered the apartment we immediately noticed a male sleeping on a couch naked from the waist down. The male was sound asleep and snoring very loudly. Officers proceeded to first try and wake the male by yelling, but he was not having it. Officers then proceeded to shake the male. The male woke up and appeared to still be drunk from clearly what had been a long night of drinking.

Officers attempted to have the male stand up to place him in handcuffs, but he became irritated and hostile, yelling and refusing to listen to officers' demands. The next thing we knew, we were in a physical fight with the male on the floor of the caller's apartment, with the family, including children, watching. Watching a cop trying to not freak out as exposed genitalia are dragging across his uniform could probably scar a child! Once we got the male handcuffed we walked him out to the patrol car. The pants, shoes and wallet that were in the hallway all belonged to the male. The male proceeded to tell us that he was at a bar just up the street earlier in the night and left around 2 a.m. The male stated that he lives close to the bar so he decided to walk home. The male did not realize that he had walked to the wrong apartment complex as his was about 2 blocks down.

I TRIED TO SAVE MY FRIEND

I was working days when I was dispatched to an alley to check on the well-being of a male that was allegedly doing CPR on a frog. Right, a frog. Upon arrival I spoke with that male and noticed he was carrying a shoe box. He was kind enough to show me the contents: a dead frog. He continued on to share about the frog being a friend of his and that he "tried to wake him up" but was unsuccessful.

EVIL MINIONS

About midnight the radio chirped. "Disturbance, unknown source of screaming," the dispatcher said. We respond to suspicious situations of unknown origin all the time. We ask questions the dispatchers cannot answer because the caller cannot answer them. So, we just find out when we get there. This was no different. So, three units started toward the residence in a well-to-do neighborhood. This is where that "other half" lives. I was first on scene and pulled into the drive. I turned on all my lights to see as there are no landscape lights on the wooded lot. As I stepped out of my car, I could hear screaming coming from behind the house. I called it in as the second car pulls in behind me. I trained my flashlight and gun on the unknown ahead of me as I traversed the vast landscape and moved toward the rear of the house. I rounded the corner and could now hear multiple voices. From within 50 feet of a swimming pool I saw what appeared to be two young men attempting to drown another one. They were on the side and their victim was in the water trying to climb out. I mustered my loudest command voice and from 10 feet or so behind them I yelled, "Police. Move your ass back from the pool! Let him out!" Shocked at my sudden presence they scurried backward away from the pool. By that time my partner had caught up with me, and covered them. I moved toward the victim. He was still in trouble, or so it seemed. I holstered up and reached out my hand to pull him out. He locked eyes with me, but instead of being assured, he screamed louder and ducked under the water and swam away from me. "Perhaps he couldn't see past my flashlight," I thought. I lowered my light so he could clearly see my uniform. That didn't help. I chased him around the pool, me on the deck, him in the water. We went round the pool a couple of laps before I heard my partner yelling at me:

"DRUGS!"
"What?"
"LSD!"
"Jesus!"

So, what appeared to be a murder in progress was actually two friends trying to pull their buddy out of the water. They had been licking "stamps" of LSD and he was tripping bad. He thought he was on fire, so he jumped into the pool to put himself out. They tried to convince him that he was not, but he believed them to be demons, so he fought them off. He was alternating between drowning himself and knocking himself out on the poolside. When he saw me he went into full panic mode. He thought I was Satan and I had come to finish the job my minions started.

Now we had to figure out how to get him out before he hurt himself. We called medics. We relied on the help of his friends since they were already wet. The plan was for them to get us just one arm so we could cuff it and pull him out. It worked, and we got him cuffed, for the time being. While in the driveway waiting on medics we let our attention lapse. It was then he jumped up. In one motion he jumped and, like using a jump rope, he swung his arms under him and got them to his front. We stood there shocked for a second until he took off running. To the back yard we went. He ran and dove from about 10 feet toward the pool. He came up short and slid across the deck, only to slide into the water. Now he was bleeding from his face. He was still "on fire" he exclaimed. My partner slid in about half way before he caught himself.

We got him out and cuffed his ankles until the gurney arrived. I followed the ambulance to the hospital and watched until the good meds kicked in. As he drifted off to sleep his mother arrived. At first she didn't believe my story, but his friends confirmed it when they got there. Their little "trip" scared the hell out of them. They had some explaining to do when their parents got home. Thankfully, no one got burned to death or drowned that night. I wish we had body cams back then because no one wanted to believe us.

OR IS IT . . .

TWO COPS, ONE BUCKET

One brisk Sunday morning at sunrise, the quietest time for police anywhere, I was talking with a beat partner in a cul-de-sac before shift change. We watched a local resident we both recognized from frequent calls walking by. About halfway down the street she turned up into an abandoned shotgun house. Being curious, we walked the few houses down to peek in the pane-less window. Right away we saw the young "lady" squatting over a 5-gallon bucket, defecating in it. She looked up and saw us looking at her. We turned and walked back down the street, both of us wishing we had minded our own business. She exited and walked toward us. As she passed and hit the cut at the end of the street she repeated, "I'm sorry. I'm sorry," about six times; we didn't respond. Think about the situation - this is America in the year 1999. She used a bucket in a random abandoned house to defecate with no paper and no running water. Sadly, she knows that's right where she can go to relieve herself. This is your average "hood" in case you didn't know. Sigh. I love my job.

Fast forward two weeks; a hot burglary call comes out. The residents were home around midnight when someone broke in to steal . . . anything. The homeowner fought with the lone suspect until he got overpowered. The suspect escaped with a VCR and ran down the street. Several units arrived with tires squealing. The homeowner pointed down the street to an abandoned house where he last saw the suspect running with the VCR under his arm like a football. We moved stealthily as ninjas to the house and made our way around it, taking quick peeks in each window. My partner spied the suspect hiding behind a broken couch, and signaled me with his flashlight to move toward the back door. As my partner entered the front door, I positioned myself to wait for the suspect to make a hasty exit out the back.

All of a sudden I heard screaming and commotion. I heard orders to show hands and then the familiar rumbling sound of people fighting on a hardwood floor. I made my entry and headed toward the sound of the struggle. I arrived in time to see my partner rolling with the suspect in the den floor. Making my way around and over all the debris in the room, I was able to grab an arm to get one cuff and

42

pull with all my might. My partner had the other arm, twisting it toward me so I could slap the second cuff on. Suddenly, in an instant of desperation, my partner threw his hands up like a calf roper looking for time. As we stood up, I saw a perplexed look on my partner's face, his nose crinkled. I asked, "Are you okay?" He picked up his light, pointed it to his chest and yelled, "IS THAT DOOKIE??!! Did I roll around in DOOKIE??!!"

Now, I was just trying to catch my breath from the fight, but it started to sink in exactly where we were. Yes, it was the same house known to locals as the place to leave your excrement, and there was the proof - the bucket - rolling a few feet away. My partner ran out of the house to the headlights of incoming units. "AAHHH!" is the cry I heard coming from outside. I grabbed the suspect and VCR and dragged him outside since he still wouldn't come willingly. The first thing I then saw was my partner running next door and turning on a hose. Our sergeant grabbed the hose and sprayed him down in full uniform! After a quick survey I saw, thankfully, that I didn't have any of said "dookie" on me. So, I started laughing to the point where I couldn't stop, probably because of the combination of the situation and that a grown man used the word "dookie" to describe feces.

Another unit came to transport the suspect while I took my partner to his house to change. It was freezing out but we rode with the windows down. I struggled to drive while hanging my head out of the window in order to avoid the smell. I laughed the whole time. My partner's uniform never went inside. He took it off and threw it into the garbage can outside. Thank goodness it was dark, because my partner was standing outside in his wet underoos holding his duty belt and boots. After he showered and changed we made it back to the station to file reports. I made sure to document my partner's words exactly, you know, to humor the folks at the magistrate's office.

BONUS: 54 TIMES WEIRD THINGS WERE FOUND IN POCKETS

1. A slime covered dildo. I'm assuming it's still lying on the side of I-70 where I chucked it instinctively.

2. A bottle of piss that he was keeping warm to take to his parole officer. However, we later found out that it was his sisters and she was pregnant, which was funny because his sister's husband had a vasectomy!! Woops.

3. A female had a whole iPhone up her you know where. Why...WHY!!!???

4. Loose laundry detergent.

5. 18 $100 bills in the pocket of a guy I arrested for stealing a $7 bottle of aspirin.

6. A mummified frog. It was his "friend."

7. A $100 bill. The guy arrested said the cash belonged to the subject . . . but the cocaine folded inside wasn't his.

8. Way back in my rookie days, this freak had several foil-wrapped balls of his own fecal matter in his pocket. What, that's not

normal?

9. A Polaroid picture of a penis. The guy wanted me to throw it away before he was booked, but he made sure to tell me "Don't worry it's not a picture of mine." Like that makes it any better for me.

10. A dildo down the front of a guy's pants. He said he was on a first date and wanted to impress her. She was in the car at the time. Somehow she was made aware of my discovery. Unknown if there was a second date.

11. Prescription bottle with unknown liquid substance inside. Arrested for DUI, Sgt. determined it was urine after giving a sniff test. Lesson is: never perform the sniff test!

12. A turtle in one pocket and a frog in another. Both alive.

13. Rolled over an arrestee and mice and bugs scurried from his pants.

14. Took a guy in one day who had an electric switch in his shirt pocket with a wire that ran from the shirt pocket and right up his bum! He said it was a pacemaker. We took him to hospital and they took the vibrator out! When he wanted a thrill he just flipped the switch in his shirt pocket!

15. $300 in the pocket of a dead man. That's not necessarily weird; however, he was homeless and aggressively panhandling. He got crabby with the wrong person who didn't give him money, knocked his belongings out of his hands, and they began to fight. In the course of the fight, he was knocked into the path of a city bus and killed. Killed for wanting to fight the wrong guy over a $1 when he had over $300.

16. I was searching a guy who had what felt like a soft football in his groin area. He insisted there was nothing there, so we did a strip search. Turns out, it was his scrotum that was bigger than a football. He said he had a hernia for years and just never got it

fixed. Lesson: get hernias fixed.

17. A handful of Oxy pills covered in dried semen. When asked "Why?" his answer was, "So nobody would wanna rob me of 'em." Yeah, that'll do it.

18. Boudin and hog's head cheese. And a cork screw. It's a Louisiana thing.

19. Wasn't in his pocket, but a dude had a piece of twine tied around his penis, with a large fishing weight hanging from the end of it. Kinda strange.

20. A plastic elephant between two slices of bread. In another pocket he had chicken bones.

21. A couple of hotdogs a guy had just stolen from a closed convenience store.

22. A pill bottle filled with someone else's urine.

23. Condoms and super glue. Didn't ask.

24. Weirdest thing I heard was 3 D-cell batteries taped to the inner thigh of a guy with wires at both ends attached to his scrotum.

25. Pat down on a homeless guy one night when a frog jumped out of his hoodie pocket. I asked him to confirm that it was actually a frog in his pocket and all he could tell me was it was his friend.

26. A used tampon stuffed inside a glass "rose tube." Yes, it came off a guy.

27. I once found a love note written on notebook paper high school style with little hearts and everything, including meth inside.

28. A mashed up potato, skin and all. My friend once found a dead snake.

29. Lube-covered chicken giblets found on a shoplifting suspect.

30. Bed bugs!!! Dead bed bugs that she said she saved every week for me. She even named them.

31. A vial of her grandpa's ashes. Tested negative for cocaine . . .

32. Dead mouse that the drunk guy swore was alive when he first put it in there.

33. A burrito and polish sausage in the same pocket. He asked if he could eat them before he went in the cell.

34. Unwrapped brownie and an emptied out chapstick tube with Viagra inside of it.

35. Guy had 6 cell phones, and a full size iPad. Yes, in one pocket.

36. I found a Taser that looked like a cell phone. I was wondering why she had two phones on her. I about zapped myself trying to shut it off.

37. On two separate occasions and on two different suspects: I found one of their teeth they had kept for some unknown reason.

38. A full set of dentures. They were not his. He "found them."

39. A big wad of raw hamburger in the front pants pocket. It had no packaging and he stated that he was "saving it for later."

40. A salt shaker with hair in it.

41. Do x-rays count?

42. A whole onion.

43. Snake in a bra!!!!

44. Hamster.

45. A voodoo doll!

46. I once had a woman that was brought to the emergency department by police for a more thorough search by a female. It turns out that she had a vine growing out of her, um, "lady parts." The doctor removed it and inquired of any reason from the woman as to why a plant was growing out of her body. The suspect answered, "My mamma said to put it there so my lady part gets tighter." The doc then asked how long it had been there? She said about 4 months since her last kid was born. Dealing with decomposition seems pleasant compared to the sight of a growing potato in a lady part for 4 months. Oh, and to make it worse, the blood test came back: she was 3 months pregnant.

47. It's not a pocket but I think this is close enough: While searching a female informant prior to a controlled narcotics buy, my partner and I had her lift up a fold of skin on her side to ensure no dope or cash was hidden underneath. A milk dud fell out and I shit you not, she picked it up and ate it.

48. A ziplock bag containing some dirt, uncooked grains of rice, and coins. My sergeant said he believed it to be used for some sort of Mexican witchcraft. Then she pulled down her pants and pissed all over the inside of my buddy's brand new Tahoe.

49. Took an entire onion out of an inmate's ass crack after a pat search revealed an "anomaly." He intended to sell it once he got it back to the housing unit.

50. Mothballs. Not candy...mothballs.

51. A dead gerbil. Thought it was a lucky rabbit's foot when I first grabbed it.

52. A fish filet. Just cut from a bluefish the day before. Smelled real good.

53. A bowl of hot soup.

54. A pound of solid uncovered bologna.

CONTACT HUMANIZING THE BADGE AT:

www.humanizingthebadge.com
www.facebook.com/humanizethebadge
humanizingthebadge@gmail.com

Made in the USA
Middletown, DE
11 December 2017